when life

takes what

matters

Devotions to Comfort You Through Crisis and Change

SUSAN LENZKES

Discovery House Publishers is affiliated with RBC Ministries,
Grand Rapids, Michigan 49512.

Discovery House books are distributed to the trade exclusively by
Barbour Publishing, Inc., Uhrichsville, Ohio 44683.

Library of Congress Cataloging-in-Publication Data

Lenzkes, Susan L.
    When life takes what matters / Susan Lenzkes.
        p.   cm.
    ISBN 0-929239-70-9
    1. Consolation—Prayer–books and devotions—English.
2. Suffering—Religious aspects—Christianity. I. Title.
BV4909.L46 1993
248.8'6—dc20   92-31268
                                     CIP

SPECIAL THANKS TO

Elsa McInnes
for your correspondence, encouragement, and love,
which have blessed me; for your life, which has encouraged me.

Anzea Publishers
for allowing me to excerpt Elsa's book Shattered and Restored.

Marilyn Anglin Anderson
for the use of your touching poem on shared joy.

Dad
for your prayers and for being courageous.

Friends and family
for praying me through the days when I was living out these pages.

Herb
for your patience when I was writing these pages.

Bob DeVries and Carol Holquist
for being there and being wonderful.

Julie Link
for being my editor and friend.

Dear ones at Discovery House Publishers
for praying as you waited for me and for this book; I love you.

My Heavenly Father
for carrying me through the loss of my
father, husband, and mother-in-law
since writing this book.

This is not an introduction; it's a prayer. A prayer gathered from days of struggling to somehow turn words and sentences into comfort and hope. A prayer for you. For this terrible loss you're facing. Or for this loss on top of all the others.

Loss comes in many shapes and sizes, but it always comes accompanied by pain and sleeplessness. This prayer was found in the rumpled sheets of a sleepless night. I have tossed and turned with you in your pain because I have tossed and turned in my own. God's Spirit yearns through me to touch you tenderly where you hurt the most.

This is a prayer of understanding, reluctantly learned in the school of loss. Some of its lessons you will find in the words of this book. Life can be very difficult.

But most importantly this prayer is portable and very persistent. It will go with you and stay with you. And for every tear that falls from your eyes, this prayer will rise again, for it is a prayer of promise.

The God of all comfort will help you. He will be patient with your pain and its process. All through your long night, He will hold you close to His heart. He will lead you and teach you gently. And when morning finally comes, you will touch yourself with wonder and find that you are healed—and that you are helping other wounded ones. All this He will do because of His great compassion. And because He loves you with an everlasting love.

Amen.

Dear Hurting One

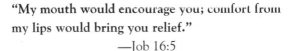

"My mouth would encourage you; comfort from my lips would bring you relief."
—Job 16:5

The measure of loss you are experiencing is
beyond my emotional comprehension.
Yet I ache with you and
long to lift your load,
even while knowing that you alone must carry
one grief at a time to
the God of all comfort.
How I pray that He will lead you
daily
to the storehouse of His
grace, compassion, and healing.

And on that day when I need
help through grief's dark night,
I pray that God will grant me the tender gift of
you.

Praise be to the God and Father of our Lord Jesus
Christ, the Father of compassion and the God of all
comfort, who comforts us in all our troubles, so that
we can comfort those in any trouble with the comfort
we ourselves have received from God. For just as the
sufferings of Christ flow over into our lives, so also
through Christ our comfort overflows.

—2 Corinthians 1:3–5

The Truth about Loss

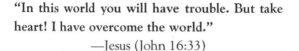

"In this world you will have trouble. But take heart! I have overcome the world."
—Jesus (John 16:33)

We *don't like it*, but we know that it's true: trouble is a natural part of living in this fallen world. The lessons come early and stay late.

As babies, we are wet and no one seems to notice. We cry and Mom doesn't rush to pick us up. Then one day we're expected to give up our warm bottle or breast for a cold hard cup. Our favorite blanket disappears in the wash. The stuffing comes out of our teddy bear. "No!" seems to be the answer for everything we want to touch or taste. Daddy keeps walking out the door, and Mommy spends too much time with that bawling little intruder. And these are the normal losses. There are worse.

As children, we find the excitement of going to school is tempered by having to leave the security of home. We learn that "F" stands for failure, not fun. We lose a friend to someone who's prettier or smarter. We are the last one picked for the team. We finally start liking the teacher, then we're promoted to the next grade. And these are the normal losses. There are worse.

As teenagers, we find that our bodies and emotions are a foreign land with ever-changing boundaries. We feel okay about ourselves only if we lose our identity to fads and fashion. A broken romance shreds our heart. Our parents don't understand us. We've lost childhood and can't find adulthood. And these are the normal losses. There are worse.

As adults, instead of celebrating the freedom we expected, we find ourselves tied to a job, a family, and a schedule. Babies cry and throw up. Kids argue and whine. Teens announce their superiority. Our grand dream for how life should be whimpers and slides sideways. People change, disappoint, fail, and leave us. Society is a mess. Gray hairs emerge. We lose our ability to lose weight. The children grow up and move out. Wrinkles and arthritis move in. We can't remember where we put our glasses. And these are the normal losses. There are worse.

We cope with these everyday losses fairly well. We adjust our attitude or change our perspective, method, or approach. Some losses we consciously grieve. Others we hardly notice because they occur so slowly. Occasionally we discover within life's process of loss and change the potential for growth, compassion, or a larger view. Sometimes we settle for simple survival. But we keep moving ahead with creative persistence. This is, after all, life. And these are life's normal losses. There are worse.

Internal losses are worse. These are the deprivations and abuses that seem to be a normal part of life, but are not. They rob us of love, trust, self-esteem, confidence, and a sense of worthiness and leave us feeling inadequate, inferior, unlovable. We bleed internally.

And what about life's land-mine losses? These are the explosions we never expected, didn't deserve, and couldn't prevent. They rip our world apart, leaving gaping holes where something, or someone, important used to be. They strike at our foundation and leave us lonely, lost, frightened, angry, insecure, and needy.

How do we deal with *these*, life's worst kind of losses?

If we're wise, we treat them with tenderness, patience, and God's help. We are hurting because we have serious wounds that need healing. And healing takes time. It also takes cooperation with God.

He whose hand formed us knows how to put us back together when life's losses have left us in pieces. Whether we are being pruned, tested, or have simply been caught in the rain that "falls on the just and the unjust," He will bring us through. He is the great Healer. He is unequaled at creating something from nothing. He even knows how to bring life from death. So certainly we can trust Him with our pain, our loss, our brokenness, our very lives.

Perhaps too it will help to realize that we are more practiced in dealing with loss than we know. After all, we've made it this far.

"For I know the plans I have for you," declares the LORD, "plans to prosper you and not to harm you, plans to give you hope and a future."

—Jeremiah 29:11

Record my lament; list my tears on your scroll—are they not in your record? —Psalm 56:8

"I have heard your prayer and seen your tears; I will heal you." —2 Kings 20:5

"I am with you and will save you," declares the LORD. *"I will restore you to health and heal your wounds."* —Jeremiah 30:11, 17

The Shape of a Question

God is more concerned about what is happening *in* me than what is happening *to* me.
—Gordon R. Bear

Life *wasn't going* the way it was supposed to go. Its continuing trouble and heartache were weighing me down with a leaden "why"-shaped question mark that wound itself around my neck. I took the question to my husband, hoping for an answer. He had none.

Of all my wise and wonderful friends, at least three can be counted on for an insightful opinion on nearly any subject, especially if asked. I asked. Not only did they have no opinion, they had no clues. One friend, the one I was positive would have some sort of an answer whether I liked it or not, said, "I'm as puzzled as you are about this."

Another friend listened as my long string of recent losses shaped itself into the giant question mark. Then she heard me stab the point at its end as I cried out, "What is God trying to tell me with all of this?"

"I'm afraid I have no answer for that," she said gently, "but may I pray for you?" And she did, right there on the phone.

It wasn't long after her loving prayer that I began to understand a rule about questioning God. If I'm asking and not seeming to get an answer, perhaps I'm asking the wrong question. Maybe it needs to be rephrased—or redirected.

My question needed both. And when I gave it some room to maneuver, I found it deliberately curving back at me and rephrasing itself. It no longer asked, What is God trying to tell me? Instead it asked, What have I been telling God by my reaction? Perhaps I've been telling Him that I don't trust Him. That I don't believe He's in control. That He's not the giver of good gifts. Or that He doesn't really have my best interest at heart.

And then the question mark relaxed its crooked posture and reformed itself into a very straight, very confident, very pointed exclamation mark. My own attitude was the problem!

It was time to put away the childish measuring stick that uses circumstances to measure the love and character of God. It was time to reaffirm the truth that God is good, holy, just, sovereign, wise, and that He is Love—pure and beautiful. So I deliberately stopped asking "why" and "what" and began to ask "how."

"How, Lord, are You going to bring good for me and glory for You out of all of this?"

I'm so glad that God's results are not limited by His raw materials! I am waiting and watching. I love the way He works—first *in* me, then *around* me.

Therefore, my dear friends . . . continue to work out your salvation with fear and trembling, for it is God who works in you to will and to act according to his good purpose.   —Philippians 2:12–13

Dear friends, don't be bewildered or surprised when you go through the fiery trials ahead, for this is no strange, unusual thing that is going to happen to you. Instead, be really glad—because these trials will make you partners with Christ in his suffering, and afterwards you will have the wonderful joy of sharing his glory in that coming day when it will be displayed. . . .

So if you are suffering according to God's will, keep on doing what is right and trust yourself to the God who made you, for he will never fail you.

—1 Peter 4: 12–13, 19 TLB

Facing
the Pain

"If I say, 'I will forget my complaint, I will change my expression, and smile,' I still dread all my sufferings."

—Job 9:27–28

> I pushed against the
> pain
> the terrible sadness
> the dreaded despair.
> I said,
> "This is no way to live.
> Life is too short.
> To be victorious
> I will rise above the pain."
> But loss said,

"This is no way to live.
Life is too short
to pretend it doesn't hurt.
To be victorious,
go through the pain
toward the promise."

Humble yourselves, therefore, under God's mighty hand, that he may lift you up in due time. Cast all your anxiety on him because he cares for you.

Be self-controlled and alert. Your enemy the devil prowls around like a roaring lion looking for someone to devour. Resist him, standing firm in the faith, because you know that your brothers throughout the world are undergoing the same kind of sufferings.

And the God of all grace, who called you to his eternal glory in Christ, after you have suffered a little while, will himself restore you and make you strong, firm and steadfast. To him be the power for ever and ever. Amen.   —1 Peter 5:6–11

This Moment

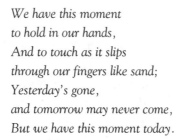

We have this moment
to hold in our hands,
And to touch as it slips
through our fingers like sand;
Yesterday's gone,
and tomorrow may never come,
But we have this moment today.

This *will be my first* Mother's Day without my mother.
Last year she was here, though just barely. It was the
last Sunday of her life.

We spent the day with her in the oncology ward.
Cancer had taken almost everything it could rob
from her body. Yet her spirit rose above the tubes and

needles, above the gaunt misery, determined to be present with her husband, children, and grandchildren—determined to give back more love than her frail body could possibly hold.

"That dress!" she rallied to say as I walked into the room. "It's the one from the catalog, the one *I* said you should order, isn't it?"

"You picked it, Mom!" I said, twirling its lavender skirt and smiling at her smiling at me. How could her eyes still have that I-love-life, I-love-pretty-things, I-love-you twinkle?

"I knew it would look great on you," she sighed, her eyes closing briefly against the heaviness of the effort to be there.

And then she received the flowers, the gifts, the words, the love, *the moment*. We knew it was all we could give her. Why hadn't we always known it?

The moment. And whatever we have in our hand and heart. That's all.

It's easy to forget that truth on ordinary days, when death is just as imminent but not so frighteningly obvious. If only we could learn to rise above the circumstances of our moments, however difficult they might be, and share heart-to-heart. Life would surely feel better, indeed, *be* better. After all, isn't this kind of love what makes Mother's Day—or any day—a celebration?

"Freely you have received, freely give."
> —Matthew 10:8

Love one another deeply, from the heart.
> —1 Peter 1:22

Speaking the truth in love, we will in all things grow up into him who is the Head, that is, Christ.
> —Ephesians 4:15

Ties of
Love

"I led them with cords of human kindness, with ties of love."

—Hosea 11:4

You've stepped across to
heaven's shore
And we are but a breath behind,
Holding dear the truth that
All that bound us close on earth
Binds us still—
For love endures forever.

My purpose is that they may be encouraged in heart and united in love, so that they may have the full riches of complete understanding. —Colossians 2:2

No one has ever seen God; but if we love one another,
God lives in us and his love is made complete in us.

We know that we live in him and he in us, because
he has given us of his Spirit. . . .

We love because he first loved us.
                                        —1 John 4:12–13, 19

All the special gifts and powers from God will someday
come to an end, but love goes on forever.
                                        —1 Corinthians 13:8 TLB

Caught Off Balance

"For I am the LORD your God, who takes hold of your right hand and says to you, Do not fear; I will help you."

—Isaiah 41:13

Sudden loss, besides leaving us hurt and bewildered, can leave us listing seriously to one side. This state of imbalance is surprising, if not downright frightening. We had no idea we were leaning so heavily on a person, job, or ability until it was yanked away without warning.

When a loved one who partially defines who we are (or who we are *not*), is taken away by death, distance, divorce, or disagreement, our grief is intensified by the loss of this part of ourselves. Maybe we had depended on the person to express emotion for us or to think or decide for us. Perhaps the person was our sense of humor, our planner, our conscience, our practical side, our memory, or even our proof of worth. In one way or another, that person was our *balance*. And now we are *off* balance.

It is not just the loss of a person that can throw us off balance. Sometimes the loss of a job, ability, ideal, attribute, or goal carries with it a large chunk of our self-esteem, identity, or purpose, leaving us feeling lopsided and ready to topple over. When this happens, it may be time to confess that our sense of well-being was improperly anchored. We may also discover that our vision needs to expand—that who we are is more than what we do or how we look, and that the sum of our worth is far more than any loss.

God's secure love and His sure promise to care for us are the perfect ballast; they provide stability without adding weight to our load. When our lives are filled with Jesus Christ and the security, worth, and identity He provides, the losses we experience cannot destabilize us.

We may still toss and turn in stormy weather, but we'll never run aground or be shipwrecked.

Find rest, O my soul, in God alone; my hope comes from him. He alone is my rock and my salvation; he is my fortress, I will not be shaken. My salvation and my honor depend on God; he is my mighty rock, my refuge. Trust in him at all times, O people; pour out your hearts to him, for God is our refuge. —Psalm 62:5–8

I waited patiently for the LORD; he turned to me and heard my cry. He lifted me out of the slimy pit, out of the mud and mire; he set my feet on a rock and gave me a firm place to stand. He put a new song in my mouth, a hymn of praise to our God. Many will see and fear and put their trust in the LORD. Blessed is the man who makes the LORD his trust, who does not look to the proud, to those who turn aside to false gods.

—Psalm 40:1–4

In Deep Shadow

We look for light, but all is darkness; for brightness, but we walk in deep shadows.
—Isaiah 59:9

Dear child of God,
when clouds descend,
when depression wraps its
heavy cloak about your soul,
when God seems distant and
you, so alone—
stretch out a finger of faith,
for you may be closer than you've
ever been . . .
He may be hiding you in the
shadow of His wing.

Beneath God's wing

deep shadow blocks our sight

and bids us hear our

darkest feelings whisper

their pain, loss, and unmet needs

into the sufficiency of God's love.

He who dwells in the shelter of the Most High will rest in the shadow of the Almighty. I will say of the LORD, "He is my refuge and my fortress, my God, in whom I trust." Surely he will save you from the fowler's snare and from the deadly pestilence. He will cover you with his feathers, and under his wings you will find refuge; his faithfulness will be your shield and rampart. You will not fear the terror of night, nor the arrow that flies by day, nor the pestilence that stalks in the darkness, nor the plague that destroys at midday. . . .

"Because he loves me," says the LORD, "I will rescue him; I will protect him, for he acknowledges my name. He will call upon me, and I will answer him; I will be with him in trouble, I will deliver him and honor him. With long life will I satisfy him and show him my salvation."   —Psalm 91:1–6, 14–16

The Unspeakable

Compassion invites the honesty that voices the unspeakable and brings healing.

I *found my little friend* hiding in a corner of the living room, kicking at the bottom of an easy chair and biting his lower lip. Clearly he had sought this lonely spot to deal with distress heavier than a three-year-old boy knew how to carry.

Kneeling beside him, I touched his shoulder. "What's the matter, Stevie?" I asked. "You seem so sad."

He turned toward the chair, covering his face with his hands, and I thought that this little one who laughed and hugged so easily was going to shut me out from his hurt. But then, with large, wet eyes, he turned and looked at me. "I'm mad with Mommy," he whispered, almost inaudibly.

"You're angry with your mommy?"

"Yes. She keeps going away. She always goes away to the hospital to be with my sister 'cause Katy's sick. But I don't *want* her to." He drew in a deep, shaky breath. "It's not good," he concluded. "It's not good for Mommy!"

"No," I agreed gently, "and not good for Stevie either, is it?"

"No, not good for Stevie either," he admitted, and then he wept without restraint.

I gathered him into my arms, rocked him and kissed him, and whispered that I knew he felt so sad. I told him how special he was and how much his mommy missed him when she had to be away to help his baby sister get over her bad sickness.

It was then, as we snuggled together, that I found myself remembering the time, months earlier, when I had felt this way.

My precious friend had been sick with cancer, and I had been sick with a malignant sorrow at the thought of losing her. Wasn't she God's faithful, loving, and fruitful servant? Didn't the world need her? And, oh, didn't *I* need her?

So I, like Stevie, had withdrawn to a lonely spot, biting my lip for control, trying to hide my sadness, and trying to hide from *God*, for I was angry with my Lord. He had the power to prevent it—but hadn't.

He found me, though, and then urged me—helped me—to cry out my rage, frustration, and indignation. At His gentle yet insistent probing, prayers too wounded to dress themselves in acceptable, respectable phrases whispered, "Unfair! Unfair!" And finally even the unspeakable was spoken—"Yes, I am angry with You!" I wept then, without restraint, feeling that He should strike me down.

As I cradled Stevie in my arms, I remembered that day and, with renewed awe, realized again that God is our Father of intimate, loving compassion. And such compassion never reacts; it responds . . . invites . . . enfolds . . . no matter what we're feeling or trying to hide.

> *It's all right—*
> *questions, pain, and*
> *stabbing anger*
> *can be poured out to*

the Infinite One and
     He will not be damaged.

Our wounded ragings will be
     lost in Him and
          we
               will
                    be
                         found.

For we beat on His chest
     from within
     the circle of His arms.

"Even now my witness is in heaven; my advocate is on high. My intercessor is my friend as my eyes pour out tears to God; on behalf of a man he pleads with God as a man pleads for his friend."   —Job 16:19–21

"Therefore I will not keep silent; I will speak out in the anguish of my spirit, I will complain in the bitterness of my soul."   —Job 7:11

I cry aloud to the LORD; I lift up my voice to the LORD for mercy. I pour out my complaint before him; before him I tell my trouble.   —Psalm 142:1–2

Sitting in Darkness

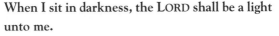

When I sit in darkness, the LORD shall be a light unto me.

—Micah 7:8 KJV

There is a place where the
    wounded soul goes to hide,
a place that cannot be reached by
    human caring,
though it nods at the effort.
    It's a dark, retractable place,
without windows and doors;
    a place where the soul would be
more alone than it has ever known
    unless Someone—

Someone able to walk through walls—
was not already there waiting.

Though the doors were locked, Jesus came and stood
among them and said, "Peace be with you!"
—John 20:26

"Peace I leave with you; my peace I give you. I do not
give to you as the world gives. Do not let your hearts
be troubled and do not be afraid." *—John 14:27*

"I have told you these things, so that in me you may
have peace. In this world you will have trouble. But
take heart! I have overcome the world."
—John 16:33

"Never will I leave you; never will I forsake you."
—Hebrews 13:5

No Simple Losses

Sometimes it takes a long, long time before we can glean enrichment from the deprivation and suffering which has baffled and overwhelmed us.

—Mildred Tengbom

"*Sure I've suffered a loss,*" you say to yourself, "and I'll admit it's been tough. But I should be able to get through this thing by now!" And you push at yourself, impatient with your progress—or seeming lack of it.

The trouble is, while you weren't looking, this *thing* you were dealing with became these *things*. Loss is never simple.

Our newly married daughter discovered this unfortunate truth when, for reasons unknown, the cartilage in her hip degenerated. Through four surgeries and two terrible years, she didn't walk a step. Simply put, Cathy lost her mobility. But that's not all she lost. Loss has a way of hemorrhaging. It bleeds into so many areas of what we do and who we are.

At a time when Cathy was just establishing her independence, she lost it. She lost her freedom (even driving a car was impossible), her hope for the future (they were not sure she would ever walk again), and thus she also lost her confidence and sense of control over her own life. She was unable to keep her job, manage her home, carry on a normal married life, or enjoy her usual pursuits. She and her new husband lost control of their finances as medical bills and worries mounted. Rather than sharing joys and hopes, she and her husband, Wes, shared struggles, fears, and disappointments.

She was no longer certain who she was. It affected all of her relationships, plans, and activities. Constant pain, interruptions for surgeries, and ongoing uncertainty left her unable to continue her college education or plan for a family. She was at the mercy of new medical techniques.

She would recover from a pioneering surgical procedure by top specialists only to be worse off than before. After one operation, she spent six weeks at our house flat on her back in a hospital bed attached to a machine that kept her leg slowly moving. There were bedpans, sponge baths, and visiting hours in our family room. Her emotional stamina deteriorated along with her physical strength. The losses were complicated and demanding. The doctors didn't know what else to do for her.

Then her doctor heard of a new technique. It had never been used in a case exactly like hers, but it might work. She was scheduled for one more surgery. When the day came, I drove for hours through rush hour traffic after leaving the cemetery where I had just watched my mother's casket being lowered into the ground. It was a day I could never have imagined. Mom was gone, and this was to be my daughter's last hope for walking.

At three o'clock in the morning, Cathy was wheeled back into her room. The weary surgeon was optimistic. It had gone well.

Months later, and for the second time in my life, I had the joy of watching my daughter take her first struggling steps. She would still need crutches, and then a cane, for a long time. But there was hope.

Time has passed. There are still limitations, but Cathy is walking again. We are all so thankful. The passage of time, however, doesn't dim the fact that those were very difficult years—made even more difficult because during that same period Wes lost three jobs due to company shutdowns, his father was killed in an auto accident, and his mother suffered two heart attacks. Loss gangs up on us sometimes.

It takes all the distance and perspective that time can afford to find the gleanings of good amid such suffering, but they are there. We are all more patient now with the complexity of loss; we understand that adjusting and healing have their own schedule.

I have watched Cathy discover who she really is and find joy wherever it is available. Things that used to upset her no longer have the same disruptive power. She knows now what's really important. She and her precious husband have grown closer through this time that tried its best to tear them apart. They are both stronger in character and coping abilities. They know that life and love are our most treasured gifts.

Today I asked Cathy what she would tell you—what she has learned through all of this. She laughed and said, "How long is this book? My whole *attitude* is different. And I'm still learning.

"You know that I've always been strong—determined." (Yes, I know!) "But now I understand that willpower alone can't always get you what you want. I had to learn to trust. And now I find that I have such compassion for people who are hurting or in trouble. I'm not quick to blame them for their condition—I just want to find a way to help.

"And I'm so thankful for the support of my family and friends. I have hope today because people cared and helped me get back on my feet!

"For a long time I was controlled by what I no longer had. Now I am able to focus on what I *do* have and be thankful. Now I treasure every moment—every experience and person. The other day I caught myself treasuring my husband *when he was in a bad mood!*"

And what would Cathy tell you as you struggle with your loss? What would *I* say to you? Be patient with yourself. Be kind to your hurts and needs. They may reach farther than you realize. Loss, after all, is not simple.

Deep calls to deep in the roar of your waterfalls; all your waves and breakers have swept over me. By day the LORD directs his love, at night his song is with me—a prayer to the God of my life. I say to God my Rock, "Why have you forgotten me? Why must I go about mourning, oppressed by the enemy?" My bones suffer mortal agony as my foes taunt me, saying to me all day long, "Where is your God?" Why are you downcast, O my soul? Why so disturbed within me? Put your hope in God, for I will yet praise him, my Savior and my God. —Psalm 42:7–11

Silent Prayers

―〜❦〜―

Be joyful in hope, patient in affliction, faithful in prayer.

—Romans 12:12

Pain is a language
without words—
and so it is untouched
by words.

Does it help to know
that my prayers for you
are often wordless too?

And shaped like tears.

In the same way, the Spirit helps us in our weakness. We do not know what we ought to pray for, but the Spirit himself intercedes for us with groans that words cannot express. And he who searches our hearts knows the mind of the Spirit, because the Spirit intercedes for the saints in accordance with God's will.

—Romans 8:26–27

Dealing with the Feelings

Those who submerge their feelings and those who cling to them like a child's 'cuddly' will self-destruct. We own our feelings in order to bring them to the healing light of Christ to be transformed.

—Elsa McInnes, *Shattered and Restored*

At times it can be more difficult to face the feelings that surround a loss than to deal with the loss itself. In the wake of a major crisis (such as the loss of a loved one, a career, or our health) strong feelings can sweep over us like a tidal wave—gut-wrenching sorrow, loneliness, fear, emptiness, despair, rage, worthlessness, helplessness, and hopelessness.

In the aftermath of life's more subtle losses (such as loss of trust, confidence, respect, support, or a cherished hope) these same feelings can take on the qualities of quicksand and slowly suck us into despair.

Having convinced us they are here to stay, these feelings demand our attention, frighten us with their intensity, and cloud our perspective. We wish we could deny them. Outrun them. Ignore them.

But they have the right to be heard and respected. While not the whole truth, they are nevertheless true from the perspective of our emotions, and they need to be dealt with tenderly, honestly, and in the light of God's complete truth. There are, however, some precautions to take when seeking to put the reality of God together with the reality of pain.

Elsa McInnes learned this. When her beloved husband died suddenly, she and her four children were left alone with their feelings of abandonment, fear, hurt, and anger. She tried to find comfort in God, but powerful emotions threatened to destroy her once vibrant faith.

In *Shattered and Restored* she writes:

"For weeks I would attend worship and receive the truth of God's love and grace and be encouraged by the songs of praise. I would hungrily grasp spiritual truth in the readings and sermon and my shattered picture of God would begin to reform. Then I would walk out of worship into loneliness and emptiness. The combined anger of five hurting people and the emotional reality of grief would stand in stark contrast to the truth I perceived in worship. I tried in vain to reassemble my picture of God. There were new pieces that wouldn't fit. The rich gold of God's word clashed with the darker pieces of my grief. The shapes wouldn't fit together. There were comfortable pieces of truth I had held and worn smooth through the years which would not interlock with the jagged new pieces of pain. At times, in order to hold onto the word of life, I tried to deny the painful reality of anger and loneliness. At other times, when emotion ran strong, I responded by denying God's word because it seemed so false in light of my feelings.

"What was I to do? It was at that time that I stumbled upon this concept of twin realities in conflict ('emotional truth' and 'spiritual truth') and how important it is to own it *all* and bring *all* to the light of Christ for reconciliation. . . .

"It is a commonly held Christian teaching that if we receive the truth of God's word into our minds, then our corrected thought patterns will tow our wayward feelings into line.

"There is one basic error in that theory. It is a self-help system allowing Christ access to our minds only while we, in presumption, seek by sheer willpower to rectify our emotional imbalance. It's not willpower we need, but Christ's transforming power. . . .

"I learned not to fear strong feelings, but to allow them to surface fully, alive and kicking into the presence of Christ, and I discovered that, as Christ poured the oil of his healing on my feelings, my doubts about him also calmed."

Thank you, dear Elsa. God restored you so beautifully. That gives the rest of us great hope.

He reached down from on high and took hold of me; he drew me out of deep waters. He rescued me from my powerful enemy, from my foes, who were too strong for me. They confronted me in the day of my disaster, but the LORD was my support. He brought me out into a spacious place; he rescued me because he delighted in me. —Psalm 18:16–19

Quotes taken from *Shattered and Restored* by Elsa McInnes, copyright © 1990, Anzea Publishers, 3–5 Richmond Road, Homebush West, NSW 2140, Australia. Used by permission.

God Created Hope

**But God demonstrates his own love for us in this:
While we were still sinners, Christ died for us.**
—Romans 5:8

*God created our eyes—
and we looked for alternatives.
He formed our ears—
and we listened to wrong voices.
He gave us feet—
and we walked away from Him into
loss, loneliness, and despair.
So God created
A Light through the darkness—
and He is the Way.
A Promise amid lies—*

and He is the Truth.
A Hope at the graveside—
and He is our Life.

But because of his great love for us, God, who is rich in mercy, made us alive with Christ even when we were dead in transgressions—it is by grace you have been saved. And God raised us up with Christ and seated us with him in the heavenly realms in Christ Jesus, in order that in the coming ages he might show the incomparable riches of his grace, expressed in his kindness to us in Christ Jesus. . . . For we are God's workmanship, created in Christ Jesus to do good works, which God prepared in advance for us to do.
—Ephesians 2:4–7, 10

Oh, God, Why?

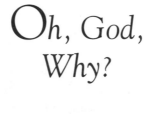

"Why have you made me your target? . . . Why
do you hide your face? . . . Why should I struggle in vain? . . . Why does the Almighty not set
times for judgment? . . . Why then did you bring
me out of the womb?"
—Job 7:20, 13:24, 9:29, 24:1, 10:18

I *have often heard it said* that people facing loss and
pain should never ask why. At best, claim the critics,
such questioning is counter-productive. At worst, it's
a sign we're not trusting God.

Why do these people say such things? Perhaps
they don't understand the question. To cry out "Oh
God, *why?*" is the natural response of a soul facing

the terrible consequences of living in a sin-filled world. The knowledge that such agony was never part of God's plan for us, and thus can never seem "right," bursts from our spirit in the form of a cry that inevitably begins with *why*.

"Why am I alone now?"

"Why is my world falling apart?"

"Why have I been betrayed?"

"Why does God seem so far away when I need Him most?"

"Why did this innocent child have to suffer and die?"

"Why is life so full of pain?"

We cling to the knowledge that God has already won the victory over death. But physical—and often painful—death is still our passageway to receive the prize of eternal life and freedom from sin's ravage.

How true that God plants seeds of hope within every thorny situation. Hope, however, does not remove life's thorns and thistles. Even though we know that loss and separation cannot harm us eternally, the hurt on this earth can at times be almost unbearable.

No one understands this better than Jesus. After hanging on a cross for three hours in utter darkness, suspended by spikes through his hands and feet while the accumulated sins of humankind were heaped upon His bleeding back, our Lord cried out through parched and swollen lips, "My God, my God, *why* have you forsaken me?"

This couldn't have been a real question from One Who had all wisdom and knowledge. He *knew* why. Together, He and the Father had built this terrifying moment of redemption into the foundation of the world! Yet His suffering, lonely spirit could not keep from crying out, "Why, God? Why? How can I bear this all alone?"

Through the tears of a loving Savior who knows the depths of what we suffer in ways we can never fathom, God hears our wrenching cries of "Oh God, *why?*"

His answers are being held tenderly in a nail-pierced hand.

"What, then, shall we say in response to this? If God is for us, who can be against us? He who did not spare his own Son, but gave him up for us all—how will he not also, along with him, graciously give us all things?
　　　　　　　　　　　　　　　　—Romans 8:31–33

"For I am convinced that neither death nor life, neither angels nor demons, neither the present nor the future, nor any powers, neither height nor depth, nor anything else in all creation, will be able to separate us from the love of God that is in Christ Jesus our Lord."

—Romans 8:38–39

Ministering Hope

The word which God has written on the brow of every man is Hope.
—Victor Hugo

The first word to wither and drop from the vocabulary of the discouraged is *hope*. Even if Victor Hugo was right when he said that God has written *hope* on my forehead, I'm still in trouble. Reading my own forehead is about as easy as kissing my own elbow.

Then along come those who mirror the love of God, and I see Hope reflected in their eyes. And that Hope, I discover, is not a thing but a person—Jesus Christ. They bring Christ to me through a helping hand, a word of encouragement, a message of love, and a touch that heals. Through such ministrations, they stretch my soul to receive the great Hope.

Christ always ministered like this—stretching shrunken souls with acts of love and compassion before imparting the large truth of who He was. And still today He is not content to settle back in the easy chair of our affection. Everywhere He looks, people are wounded and weary—giving up hope. He longs to go on ministering His Hope through us.

May you always be doing those good, kind things which show that you are a child of God, for this will bring much praise and glory to the Lord.
—Philippians 1:11 TLB

Each one should use whatever gift he has received to serve others, faithfully administering God's grace in its various forms. If anyone speaks, he should do it as one speaking the very words of God. If anyone serves, he should do it with the strength God provides, so that in all things God may be praised through Jesus Christ.
—1 Peter 4:10–11

We have this hope as an anchor for the soul, firm and secure. *—Hebrews 6:19*

Cleansing the Wound

The treatment the wound gets determines whether time will bring healing or hate.
—Elsa McInnes, *Shattered and Restored*

When *something of worth* is taken from us, we are injured. If we lose something badly needed, highly valued, or deeply loved, the wound will be deep. If it was ripped away without warning, the laceration is jagged and raw. If it was slowly scraped away, the abrasion burns and stings.

Such wounds have one thing in common. They *hurt.* We don't like the pain, but it serves a purpose; it reminds us to treat and protect our injury. A thorough cleansing prevents serious infection, and a protective bandage shields the wound from further damage.

Emotional wounds demand the same careful attention as physical wounds, and the wounds of loss are especially vulnerable to contamination.

After the shock of losing her husband to cancer, Elsa McInnes discovered the painful truth that deep wounds can be breeding grounds for very unwelcome pests. She found that her normal and predictable emotions of sorrow, fear, and anger became infected with self-pity, blame, bitterness, and resentment. She writes:

"Lord, . . . I marvel at the gentle distinction you made as you helped me face the contamination. You never once called grief a sin. You made a distinction between sin and the emotional wound that caused it. You showed me that you bind and heal emotional wounds with deep compassion. But then you gently pointed out that you can't treat destructive attitudes that find entry through those wounds the same way. There was no point in bathing them. They needed eviction notices and since the house they resided in was mine, it rested with me to tell them they were not welcome. Lord, right then I caught an uncomfortable glimpse of the wounds I was inflicting on your Holy Spirit as you tried to bandage mine."

Elsa's words hint that we may have work to do even while we are still dealing with pain, loss, and grief. We need to remain alert and close to God lest the Enemy find opportunity in our sorrow.

We may need to forgive something that seems unforgiveable. We may need to remind ourselves of how much God has forgiven us. Forgiveness begins with a choice and continues with daily, hourly, perhaps even moment-by-moment affirmations until it stands free—until *we* stand free.

We may be required to let go with grace when the time comes; to release what is being taken from us as well as the pain the loss leaves in its place. We may have to consciously choose healing and restoration and then to verbalize what we want and need God to do for us. As we begin to express our desire to be whole and seek to obey His Word, we can rest in the truth that He knows what is best for us. He knows that we need cleansing, protection, healing, and restoration. He knows that we need *Him*.

"For I am the LORD who heals you."
                                                                    —*Exodus 15:26*

When Jesus saw him lying there and learned that he had been in this condition for a long time, he asked him, "Do you want to get well?"   —John 5:6

Cleanse me with hyssop, and I will be clean; wash me, and I will be whiter than snow.   —Psalm 51:7

Let all who take refuge in you be glad; let them ever sing for joy. Spread your protection over them, that those who love your name may rejoice in you.

—Psalm 5:11

Saying Good-bye

Hearts don't have to stand close to join hands.

One of the most heartrending moments of life comes when close friends say good-bye, knowing that many miles will separate them from their countless shared experiences. Distance takes on the menacing look of an enemy when it dares to stand between such friends!

Soon they will be building protective shields around the ache of separation. They will feel themselves both courting and resisting the urge to clip those taut threads that bind their hearts in love. And they will argue repeatedly with a voice that warns,

"Don't build new friendships—life has a demolition crew around every corner!"

But discovery lies ahead. Real friendship is resilient. The very cords that made it strong—commitment, creativity, caring, and sharing—are elastic, and friends can remain committed and even more creative in their long-distance sharing.

Now cards and letters—stackable memories to be relived over a cup of coffee—will communicate love in indelible ink. Now calls—where the value of every word, enhanced by the coming bill—will set precious priorities and release sentiment from the soul. Anticipated visits will be far richer for their infrequency. Thoughts and feelings long saved and protected will be unlocked and shared.

Best of all, a discovery will be made that hearts in harmony can carry a lovely tune long distance.

Even though I am not physically present, I am with you in spirit.   *—1 Corinthians 5:3*

All my prayers for you are full of praise to God! When I pray for you, my heart is full of joy . . . How natural it is that I should feel as I do about you, for you have a very special place in my heart. We have shared to-

gether the blessings of God . . . Only God knows how deep is my love and longing for you—with the tenderness of Jesus Christ. My prayer for you is that you will overflow more and more with love for others, and at the same time keep on growing in spiritual knowledge and insight. —Philippians 1:3–4, 7–9 TLB

What Helps, What Hurts?

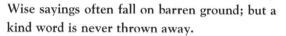

Wise sayings often fall on barren ground; but a kind word is never thrown away.
> —Sir Arthur Helps

Sensitivity to others often comes at considerable expense. Ask those who have lost a loved one or some important aspect of their life if they are now wiser regarding what helps and what hurts the grieving heart. They will know.

They will explain that God's love reaches out most tangibly through people who understand that

- they are not required to fix the hurt.
- curiosity is not the same as caring.

- a gentle touch can mean more than a great truth.
- God understands our questions and even our anger.
- a listening ear brings more comfort than the wisest mouth.
- people don't hurt less just because you tell them someone else hurts more.
- similar experiences give empathy but we can't know *exactly* how another person feels.
- people who add practical help to their prayers are an answer to prayer.
- words of love are words of encouragement.
- small acts of kindness are not small.
- all of the Scripture we know may not need to be quoted right now.
- losing one's balance is not the same as losing one's testimony.
- it takes time to live our questions all the way through to God's answers.
- time alone has no power to heal—God alone does.

Therefore, as God's chosen people, holy and dearly loved, clothe yourselves with compassion, kindness, humility, gentleness and patience. . . . And over all these virtues put on love, which binds them all together in perfect unity. —Colossians 3:12, 14

Carry each other's burdens, and in this way you will fulfill the law of Christ. —Galatians 6:2

Blessed is [s]he who is kind to the needy.
—Proverbs 14:21

When Hope Is Crushed

Losing hope, painful as it may seem, is the way to discover hope.
—David Augsburger, *When Enough Is Enough*

As *we stood chatting* after a meeting, a beautifully dressed woman of about fifty told me how deeply she was hurting. She hadn't known life could be so painful.

Until recently life had gone pretty much according to her plan. In fact, she had never been able to understand people who couldn't make life turn out right. She had met and married the perfect man, had sons who would make anyone proud, kept up a lovely home, attended church every Sunday, and found a nice job when the kids were grown. She had the formula: Live right and God will bless you with this kind of life. There was little she hoped for—except that life would continue to be this comfortable.

But it didn't. The bottom dropped out of her life and landed hard, crushing her hope for a perfect, pain-free existence.

When hope shatters, no matter how unrealistic it was, we become vulnerable to dangerous new hopes. For example, we may start to hope that, at the very least, we can rise above the pain. Isn't that what victorious living is all about? After all, God promised that we shall "mount up with wings like eagles" (Isaiah 4:31 TLB).

But life may clip the wings of even that hope, forcing us to walk the pathway covered by splinters of crushed hope. Soon our feet are sore and bleeding. At this point some folks, unable to see an end to the pathway of pain, settle for a scaled-down version of hope—a prescription that promises relief for inflamed feet. This hope expects relief—demands it in fact, reasoning that it's the very least God could do. This hope has been known to plan, scheme, bargain, demand, and even use Scripture out of context in an effort to twist the arm of God. This hope leads directly to disillusionment.

True hope focuses not on plans and prescriptions but on the person of God.

This living hope takes root in the reality of pain and holds us close to our Father who "did not spare his own Son, but gave him up for us all" (Romans 8:32).

This honest hope keeps its eyes wide open and its feet firmly planted in God's unfailing promises. All of them.

This patient hope does not demand to soar; it gratefully settles for "walking without fainting."

This sustaining hope opens the door to God's healing for my hurt, God's purpose through my pain, God's rest in my struggle, God's Word for my questions, and God's peace in the midst of my storm.

This eternal hope leads directly to heaven.

False hope expects to find relief *from* suffering. True hope expects to find God *in* suffering.

And hope does not disappoint us, because God has poured out his love into our hearts by the Holy Spirit, whom he has given us. —Romans 5:5

Let us draw near to God with a sincere heart in full assurance of faith, having our hearts sprinkled to cleanse us from a guilty conscience and having our bodies washed with pure water. Let us hold unswervingly to the hope we profess, for he who promised is faithful.
                                        —Hebrews 10:22–23

So do not throw away your confidence; it will be richly rewarded. You need to persevere so that when you have done the will of God, you will receive what he has promised.   *—Hebrews 10:35–36*

May the God of hope fill you with all joy and peace as you trust in him, so that you may overflow with hope by the power of the Holy Spirit.   *—Romans 15:13*

As the Calendar Turns

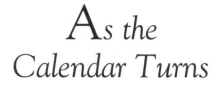

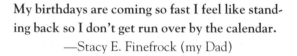

My birthdays are coming so fast I feel like standing back so I don't get run over by the calendar.
—Stacy E. Finefrock (my Dad)

A *wise old woman* once chided me for bemoaning my first gray hairs. (This, unfortunately, is not a recent story.) "Honey," she said. "Don't complain about gray hairs. Turning gray is the only part of aging that doesn't hurt!"

Another time I overheard a stooped old gentleman talking with a friend. "When I was a boy I used to wonder why old men leaned over like this when they walked," he said. "Now I know. If you try to stand up straight, you just go on over backwards!"

These people weren't comedians; they were sages.

We can all remember the days when we actually looked forward to birthdays, eagerly counting the weeks and days until we would turn a year older. "Mama, how long till I can hold up my thumb too?" (In less figurative language, this means "When will I be *five*?") And the day after we turned 15, we were already "almost 16."

Youth celebrates each year as a credit, deferring or ignoring the debit. As the years go on, we continue to celebrate the gains and laugh at the losses. We are preoccupied with living, and that's good.

Then someone speeds up the clock. The smoke over the birthday cake barely clears before it's time to blow out the candles again. And the strains of "Happy Birthday to You" start up again while last year's verse is only half finished, like a Sunday school chorus sung in rounds.

This is when time begins whispering her not-so-subtle suggestion that we have failed to understand her. Our understanding grows, however, when we begin paying the price in our own bodies or watching parents or friends pay it in theirs. We can no longer ignore the fact that we are breaking down, wearing out, falling apart, and losing control.

The rate of deterioration seems to depend on health, heredity, and how well we have cared for ourselves. The *perceived* rate of deterioration may depend more on attitude; the ability to cover up, adjust, and compensate; and whether or not some important parts of us are growing rather than diminishing.

As the calendar pages turn with ever-increasing speed—robbing us of vigor, agility, strength, and energy; passion, endurance, stature, and health; smooth skin, thick hair, keen sight, and sharp hearing; dexterity, balance, skill, and memory—we know where to find comfort. As we follow, love, and obey our Lord, His character will grow stronger within us, blessing us with maturity, perspective, faith, wisdom, love, patience, endurance, peace, and joy, no matter how weak our bodies become. How blessed we are to have our hope built on that which time cannot take away.

But we have this treasure in jars of clay to show that this all-surpassing power is from God and not from us. . . . Therefore we do not lose heart. Though out-

wardly we are wasting away, yet inwardly we are being renewed day by day. For our light and momentary troubles are achieving for us an eternal glory that far outweighs them all. So we fix our eyes not on what is seen, but on what is unseen. For what is seen is temporary, but what is unseen is eternal.

Now we know that if the earthly tent we live in is destroyed, we have a building from God, an eternal house in heaven, not built by human hands. Meanwhile we groan, longing to be clothed with our heavenly dwelling, because when we are clothed, we will not be found naked. For while we are in this tent, we groan and are burdened, because we do not wish to be unclothed but to be clothed with our heavenly dwelling, so that what is mortal may be swallowed up by life. Now it is God who has made us for this very purpose and has given us the Spirit as a deposit, guaranteeing what is to come. Therefore we are always confident and know that as long as we are at home in the body we are away from the Lord. We live by faith, not by sight.

—2 Corinthians 4:7, 16–18; 5:1–7

Multiplied Sorrows

I add to my troubles when I treat myself even worse than my loss is treating me.

Left to itself, life does a fair amount of dividing and subtracting. Death and distance divide. Divorce and disagreement divide. Many treasured things are subtracted from our lives by decay, disease, deception, desertion, depravity, and the other effects of sin in this world. In spite of our best efforts, we often find ourselves on the losing end of life.

So why do we add to our own sorrows?

Unconsciously, we compare ourselves to someone who is better off, and we feel worse. Or we blame ourselves for doing what we did or for not doing what we should have done or could have done. The "if onlys" set up headquarters in our hearts. Anger boils until it hardens into resentment, bitterness, and unforgiveness. We jump to conclusions, feed negative thoughts, make assumptions, anticipate and predict the worst. And we bombard ourselves with an endless volley of depressing messages:

- I can't survive or ever be happy again without this thing/person.
- I will never get through this.
- I must be a failure/bad/hopeless.
- The rest of my life is going to be miserable.
- I have been singled out for abuse.
- I will always feel this afraid/vulnerable/angry/depressed.
- God has deserted me.
- I can't make it through one more night.
- No one can help.

If we catch ourselves in the act of saying, doing, or believing such things, we have an opportunity to tell ourselves the truth instead.

- Yes I hurt, but I will not hurt forever.
- Even pain has a beginning, a middle, and an end.
- I will survive.

- God does care.
- Some of God's people know how to comfort me.
- Even if this is my fault, beating myself won't help.
- God loves me tenderly when I'm hurting.
- I can't see it through these tears, but God does have a future for me.
- Morning will come.

Let the wise listen and add to their learning.
                                          —Proverbs 1:5

Each of you must put off falsehood and speak truthfully.   *—Ephesians 4:25*

Do not add to what I command you and do not subtract from it.   *—Deuteronomy 4:2*

Live as children of light (for the fruit of the light consists in all goodness, righteousness and truth) and find out what pleases the Lord.   *—Ephesians 5:8–10*

Now may the Lord of peace himself give you peace at all times and in every way. —2 Thessalonians 3:16

Who Betrayed Whom?

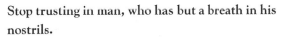

Stop trusting in man, who has but a breath in his nostrils.

—Isaiah 2:22

I looked to you, my friend,
I trusted in you and
counted on your strength,
balance, and wisdom.
I believed in you!
Because you proved human,
because you fell,
does that make you a failure?
And does it mean I have been betrayed?
Or does it simply mean that I
heaped upon your slender shoulders

the burden of idealism—
that I placed you on the pedestal of
my high standards and
chained your feet with heavy links
of expectation?
Did I ask you to be God
and then weep when you were not?

For who is God besides the LORD? And who is the Rock except our God? —Psalm 18:31

It is better to take refuge in the LORD than to trust in man. It is better to take refuge in the Lord than to trust in princes. —Psalm 118:8–9

"Blessed is the man who trusts in the LORD, whose confidence is in him. He will be like a tree planted by the water that sends out its roots by the stream. It does not fear when heat comes; its leaves are always green. It has no worries in a year of drought and never fails to bear fruit." —Jeremiah 17:7–8

"For the LORD God, my God, is with you. He will not fail you or forsake you." —1 Chronicles 28:20

The Gift
of Laughter

I believe that laughter is a sacred sound to our
God.

—Tim Hansel, *You Gotta Keep Dancin'*

Not all laughter comes easily. There is a laughter that
waits to be born. It is laughter at the end of
exhaustion . . . laughter after pain . . . laughter for the
joy of release . . . earned laughter . . . laughter all the
brighter for its stark background . . . laughter stitched
together with that ragged yet tough filament we call
faith (or is it endurance?) . . . laughter that knows every note in the scale of life by heart—all its highs and
lows—yet sings out its lilting tune anyway.

This laughter is more than just a sound, more than mirth, more than any comedian has ever hoped to evoke. It is the soul bubbling over with hope and victory. It is the voice of joy. Like a magnet it draws every scrap of life within its radius toward the promise of living, loving, and trusting.

Life does demand that we cry—often. But we need to laugh still more often. Because there will be an end to our tears, but never to our joy!

> *There is a time for everything, and a season for every activity under heaven: . . . a time to weep and a time to laugh, a time to mourn and a time to dance.*
> —*Ecclesiastes 3:1, 4*

> *"Blessed are you who weep now, for you will laugh."*
> —*Luke 6:21*

> *Those who sow in tears will reap with songs of joy. He [she] who goes out weeping, carrying seed to sow, will return with songs of joy, carrying sheaves with him [her].*
> —*Psalm 126:5–6*

Losing an
Argument

**You can learn many things from children. How
much patience you have, for instance.**
—Franklin P. Jones

One of life's most unforgettable experiences is to en-
gage in any sort of discussion (i.e., argument) with a
teenager defending his or her autonomy with the
newfound weapons of reason and logic. It ranks right
up there with being in a rear-end collision.

During the discussion you won't understand
where you're going, and when it's over you won't
know where you are or how you got there. Or why it's
costing you so much money. It's worse than being
audited by the IRS.

For one thing, teenagers approach discussions convinced that they hold insights discovered sometime after you last comprehended anything—if indeed you ever did. For another thing, they refuse to honor the age-old parental logic that says, "Because it's my house and that's the way I want it." Or, "Because I'm the parent and I'm paying the bills . . ."

They say, "But wait, just *think* about it a minute," leaning heavily on the word *think* as though dangling a fresh carrot before a starving rabbit. And, "Be *reasonable!*" Which means, "No one with half a brain would disagree with me about this!"

A newly emerging adult may promise to take you on a trip from point A to point C, but en route you will inevitably pass through I-can't-believe-you-are-this-ignorant-of-the-real-issue! It is not a nice place to visit.

From my perspective, the *real* issue is how I got into this situation in the first place. I would hate to have to explain to the kid that if I were a truly logical person, I would never have become a *mother*.

But I did choose to become a mother. And as I see it, patiently loving my children through every stage, however difficult, is the way to win while seeming to lose.

How else can a logical person look at it?

"What ails you that you keep on arguing? . . ." When will you end these speeches? Be sensible, and then we can talk. . . . "I waited while you spoke, I listened to your reasoning; while you were searching for words, I gave you my full attention."
—Job 16:3, 18:2, 32:11–12

The end of a matter is better than its beginning, and patience is better than pride. Do not be quickly provoked in your spirit, for anger resides in the lap of fools. Do not say, "Why were the old days better than these?" For it is not wise to ask such questions. . . . Do not pay attention to every word people say.
—Ecclesiastes 7:8–10, 21

Take note of this: Everyone should be quick to listen, slow to speak and slow to become angry, for man's anger does not bring about the righteous life that God desires.
—James 1:19–20

Above all, love each other deeply, because love covers over a multitude of sins.
—1 Peter 4:8

Puzzling over Change

Most people resist change, and yet it's the only thing that brings progress.

—From *Live and Learn and Pass It On*

If I'm going to ponder some great philosophical mystery, I want to pick a meaningful subject. I'd prefer not to spend my time arguing whether the chicken or the egg came first. Let somebody else figure that one out and save me the trouble. I'll work on my own puzzles.

My thorny question for this week is, Does change produce loss or does loss produce change? And if (as I strongly suspect) the answer is both, then which came first, the chicken or the egg?

I'm sorry. I shouldn't toy with a subject this serious. As necessary as change is to life and progress, it can be very difficult. Even positive change can be tough—even change that we choose.

Get married and you gain a spouse and the chance for a lifetime of love and sharing. But you lose your privacy, quite a bit of your freedom, and several arguments as well.

Have a baby and you'll be changing more than the wallpaper in what you used to call the den. You'll also change about four thousand diapers and several lofty standards. And you'll lose your heart, your sleep, and most of your hair before the kid is grown.

Move to a new house and you can lose your way to the bathroom in the night. If you relocate in a new town you lose everything from church family and friends to your favorite hamburger stand and the only person who knew how to cut your hair.

If you accept a new job, you may leave behind an annoying boss or co-worker, but you also lose your familiar position and duties.

But we don't have the luxury of choosing all of the changes that come our way. And some of the changes are frightening and difficult.

Last year my husband was among those who lost their jobs when the defense industry had to shrink to match its meager new budget. After twenty-nine years of going to work every day for the same company, Herb had nowhere to go. Our youngest had moved out just prior to Herb's layoff, so there we were, just the two of us.

There was plenty to worry about, and we could have passed the worries back and forth in an endless tournament of despair. But for some wonderful reason we didn't, opting instead to trust God and enjoy our time together. We did a lot of talking, sorting of priorities, playing, and catching up on projects around the house. God knew all of the problems and needs we were facing. He was just as aware as we were that if Herb wasn't re-hired he would lose most of his early retirement package. We decided to do what we could and leave the rest with God.

As it turned out, Herb was hired back after a couple of months, but the only job they could find for him was as a mechanical engineer. He is an *electronics* engineer. He has a master's degree in how to chase invisible electrons, not in how to repair hardware! But the company offered no schooling. Just new responsibilities and new problems.

Fortunately, my husband chooses to see change as a challenge. And what a challenge this was! He had all new jargon to learn, new concepts and new people to deal with. He was no longer in charge; he was taking orders from someone else. One day he sat at his desk looking at an elaborate sketch he had drawn while standing on the third level of a scaffold looking at the inside of a plane fuselage which was upside down and backwards. *Who drew this?* he groaned, looking at the intricate maze. *And whatever does it mean?*

But he kept at it and met the challenge, turning his losses into gains. He actually began to have fun learning and growing through it all. For while it's true that change sometimes brings loss, and loss inevitably brings change, change also brings opportunities for progress and *growth*. Or is it that growth always brings change? Sounds like a good puzzle for next week!

"Forget the former things; do not dwell on the past. See, I am doing a new thing! Now it springs up; do you not perceive it? I am making a way in the desert and streams in the wasteland . . . to give drink to my

people, my chosen, the people I formed for myself that they may proclaim my praise." —Isaiah 43:18–21

Every good and perfect gift is from above, coming down from the Father of the heavenly lights, who does not change like shifting shadows. —James 1:17

Faith's
Last Leap

I have fought the good fight, I have finished the race, I have kept the faith.

—2 Timothy 4:7

The *day after* my mother died, I was leafing through her favorite daily devotional guide when I came across a loose page torn and saved from some other book.

Carefully removing it, I read of a young boy's experience writing and mailing his very first letter. Painstakingly he had printed, "Dear Grandpa," and then spelled out what he wanted for his birthday. At last, satisfied with the wording of his request, he put his letter in an envelope and walked with his mother to the mailbox. She lifted him up and said, "Let it go." The boy hesitated. Would Grandpa really receive the letter if he dropped it into the big, dark box? But he did let go, and when the young boy received his grandfather's present he also received his first lesson in trust.

As I sat there I recalled my dear mother's *last* lesson in trust. I had watched her struggle between hanging on to this life and letting go of it—struggle against leaving this earth and the people she loved so dearly—repeatedly fighting her way back from the banks of the River Jordan for one more kiss, one more smile, one more touch, just one more "I love you."

It must take a lot of faith to let go when God says it is time to cross the dark chasm that separates the earthly life we know from the unknown glories beyond. It is faith's last great effort. But when we do, how swiftly faith must become sight and darkness become eternal light.

Right now, as I speculate as to the glories of heaven and the beauty of the Savior who gave Himself as a ransom for us, I can see my mother looking into His eyes. And if I know her, she's roaming through gardens of delight arm in arm with Him, exclaiming over fragrances she never dreamed existed and admiring colors that He didn't put in our rainbow.

> *Praise be to the God and Father of our Lord Jesus Christ! In his great mercy he has given us new birth into a living hope through the resurrection of Jesus Christ from the dead, and into an inheritance that can never perish, spoil or fade—kept in heaven for you, who through faith are shielded by God's power until the coming of the salvation that is ready to be revealed in the last time. In this you greatly rejoice, though now for a little while you may have had to suffer grief in all kinds of trials. These have come so that your faith—of greater worth than gold, which perishes even though refined by fire—may be proved genuine and may result in praise, glory and honor when Jesus Christ is revealed.* —1 Peter 1:3–7

He Is
Our Hope

Christ in you, the hope of glory.
—Colossians 1:27

*Sometimes the very best of life is
removed from sight and touch
and we are left behind to
cling to one another and
hope in Him Who
loved us
and gave Himself for an
eternity with
no good-byes.*

*For the Lord himself will come down from heaven,
with a loud command, with the voice of the archangel*

and with the trumpet call of God, and the dead in Christ will rise first. After that, we who are still alive and are left will be caught up together with them in the clouds to meet the Lord in the air. And so we will be with the Lord forever. Therefore encourage each other with these words. —1 Thessalonians 4:16–18

When Christmas Isn't Welcome

Like one who takes away a garment on a cold day, or like vinegar poured on soda, is one who sings songs to a heavy heart.
—Proverbs 25:20

If only holidays would have the grace to know when *not* to happen.

One brave woman I know, in spite of her staggering and relentless collection of heavy losses, went out and purchased lovely Christmas cards. She stamped and addressed them, wrote personal notes in each one, and then found she couldn't bring herself to mail them. So she tossed them all into the garbage and watched the trash collector take them away.

After a painful year it's hard to send messages of peace and good will to all. Christmas isn't welcome when it glibly promises cozy togetherness and pre-packaged joy that it can't deliver. Parties and bright lights cannot dismiss the darkness of crisis, trauma, pain, and death.

And yet God sent the Light of the World into such darkness. All around there was oppression, sickness, and suffering.

Christmas wasn't welcomed then either. It was shunted into the dark corner of a dank stable. Yet the animals, along with the weary and wondering new mother and her husband, found they were not blinded by the light of His glory. He left His brilliance behind and came with a soft cry into the night. Only a lantern lit the face of God.

Had it not been for the angels and the star, no one would have guessed that God had come to earth . . . except for those who sensed the love glowing in that dark place. Christmas came amid pain and poverty, loss and loneliness.

When we can't say "Merry Christmas," perhaps we can whisper, "Welcome, Light of the World. Never has the light of your presence been more needed. Shine softly in my darkness."

"The people living in darkness have seen a great light; on those living in the land of the shadow of death a light has dawned." —Matthew 4:16

He has sent me to bind up the brokenhearted, to proclaim freedom for the captives and release from darkness for the prisoners . . . to comfort all who mourn, and provide for those who grieve in Zion—to bestow on them a crown of beauty instead of ashes, the oil of gladness instead of mourning, and a garment of praise instead of a spirit of despair. —Isaiah 61:1–3

"I will lead the blind by ways they have not known, along unfamiliar paths I will guide them; I will turn the darkness into light before them and make the rough places smooth. These are the things I will do; I will not forsake them." —Isaiah 42:16

Unshared Joy

My comfort in my suffering is this: Your promise preserves my life.

—Psalm 119:50

When you were taken
so was my joy in living,
for even those things which would now
give joy
cannot be shared with you,
And there is sorrow in unshared joy.
Joy is giving and receiving.
When one is taken away who shared
in such a relationship,
the other must learn to give and receive
in other ways.

There are thoughts and events
special only to each other.
And the emptiness of no longer sharing
turns into loneliness.
Only You can meet my loneliness, O God.
Only You know where my feet have been,
where I now stand
and where I am going.
So I trust in you
and share with you completely.
To you I give
and from you I receive.
And once again
I know the meaning of joy.

When my spirit grows faint within me, it is you who know my way. . . . Look to my right and see; no one is concerned for me. I have no refuge; no one cares for my life. I cry to you, O LORD; I say, "You are my refuge, my portion in the land of the living." Listen to my cry, for I am in desperate need. —Psalm 142:3–6

My help comes from the LORD, the Maker of heaven and earth. He will not let your foot slip—he who watches over you will not slumber; indeed, he who watches over Israel will neither slumber nor sleep. The LORD watches over you—the LORD is your shade at your right hand; the sun will not harm you by day, nor the moon by night. The LORD will keep you from all harm—he will watch over your life; the LORD will watch over your coming and going both now and for-evermore. —Psalm 121:2–8

Let the morning bring me word of your unfailing love, for I have put my trust in you. Show me the way I should go, for to you I lift up my soul.
—Psalm 143:8

The Morning
of Eternity

"See, I have engraved you on the palms of my hands."

—Isaiah 49:16

Probably *no clouds* were more threatening than those that gathered above Christ's cross. All of creation must have rushed into mourning for the shame of it—that their Creator, the One whose hands had formed the earth and heavens, should have those hands pierced with nails by those He created.

But deep inside the clouds' darkness, lightning glory gathered, waiting to burst forth in victory, waiting to split the dark veil of sin hanging between God and His beloved creation.

Has ever such a silver lining been spoken as "It is finished"?

Perhaps only "He is risen!"

Oh, world, trace with joy the silver lining that will never tarnish. Tell it everywhere!

RISEN!

is

He!

The angel said to the women, "Do not be afraid, for I know that you are looking for Jesus, who was crucified. He is not here; he has risen, just as he said. Come and see the place where he lay. Then go quickly and tell his disciples: 'He has risen from the dead and is going ahead of you into Galilee. There you will see him.' Now I have told you." —Matthew 28:5–7

W ise
Sayings

**May all the wonderful things I will say about
you after you are gone be found, complete, in the
thesaurus of our todays.**

The grief of loss is a heavy load. Pity those who find
themselves adding regret to its burden. The "if onlys"
can tip the scales and unbalance us if we're not careful.

With each new day God offers us opportunities
to prevent regret. *Today* we can speak encouragement and voice our feelings. If we do it now and say
it now, we are practicing the wisdom of kindness.

I have long held a motto that if I think a kind
thought about someone—anything at all—and do

not pass it on, I am wasting diamonds. Yet, regrettably, I find I have waste cans filled with them. The kind thoughts that form in us, yet are never shaped into words or acts, may prove to be the squandering of our most valuable human resource.

Today let me tell you, my friend, that your laugh is as much fun for me as it is for you—that your tears land in my heart—that tea with you is always sweeter—that knowing you are there for me is better than owning the national treasury.

Today let me say, my child, that I see greatness in you   that I love seeing life through your eyes—that you are growing evidence of God's goodness to me— and that I sometimes look at you and congratulate myself.

Today let me tell you, my husband, that I have experienced God's tender love through you—that I'm asking God to give you a star for every back rub you've given me—that I admire the way you turn problems into challenges—and that your steady, faithful character is the most beautiful love letter ever written.

Today let me tell you, my heavenly Father, that I am rich because of You—that I stand in awe of Your creativity every time I give You one of my tangled messes—that You are altogether beautiful—and that I love the family You are building for Yourself. Thank you for letting me be part of it!

> A word aptly spoken is like apples of gold in settings of silver.   —Proverbs 25:11

> A wise man's heart guides his mouth, and his lips promote instruction. Pleasant words are a honeycomb, sweet to the soul and healing to the bones.
>   —Proverbs 16:23–24

> From the fruit of his lips a man is filled with good things as surely as the work of his hands rewards him.
>   —Proverbs 12:14

A Friend in Need

A friend loves at all times, and a brother [sister] is born for adversity.

—Proverbs 17:17

Friendship gives a license to show up at the door of need without asking "When would you like me to come?" or "What would you like me to do?" Friendship does not call out, "Just let me know if you need anything." True friendship whispers, "I'm here," and, with sensitivity, respect, and understanding, promptly steps through the door.

But what about honoring the right to invite? Those who wait for parchment invitations wait long, for need rarely throws a party—rarely even has a voice.

Yet need has its own needs. It needs protection from strangers who tromp in with work boots and good intentions. And it needs relief from acquaintances wearing the spiked heels of advice and pat answers.

Need waits with longing for the entrance of dear ones who, on ordinary days, pad barefoot through the soul.

"Oh, that I had someone to hear me!" —Job 31:35

"A despairing man [or woman] should have the devotion of his friends, even though he [she] forsakes the fear of the Almighty." —Job 6:14

The Lift of Music

When words leave off, music begins.
—Heinrich Heine

Living can be a hard business. It can strip away our resources. We can lose confidence, patience, perspective, and even our sense of humor. When this happens we urgently need to find those gifts with the power to rejuvenate.

God hides these spirit-lifters everywhere—in His nature, in His Word, in prayer, in someone's arms, in a healthy cry or a hearty laugh. But for unparalleled restorative power, music is hard to beat. It seems to be the heart's native tongue.

How often I have sat cross-legged between the speakers of my stereo, singing or just letting harmony wrap itself around my wounds and weariness. How often I have dragged myself to a rehearsal or performance and later skipped away restored. How often I have joined other voices in worship and praise and been lifted into the presence of God. Music has power to elevate, speak, soothe, teach, touch, energize, and unify.

Melody adds wings to words and flies them over obstacles that stand in the way of understanding. Within its measures music carries a large measure of comprehension. Somehow we can believe love that serenades us. Somehow we can hear hope that sings to us in the dark.

Yet even if music could do none of these things, it would still give soaring voice to our praise. And as we lift songs of worship we too will be lifted. That's the promise of praise.

Declare the praises of him who called you out of darkness into his wonderful light. —1 Peter 2:9

Sing for joy to God our strength; shout aloud to the God of Jacob! Begin the music, strike the tambourine, play the melodious harp and lyre. —Psalm 81:1–2

Pain

He has seen but half the universe who never has
been shewn the house of Pain.
>—Ralph Waldo Emerson

> *My life is*
> *Your song, dear Lord,*
> *And if You choose to*
> *write that song,*
> *in part,*
> *in minor key,*
> *give voice to sing despite*
> *the taste of tears.*
> *With hands hard-clasped*
> *in pain,*
> *and head bowed low*
> *in trust,*

I know You hear such
minor songs
as major praise.

My eyes are ever on the LORD, for only he will release
my feet from the snare. Turn to me and be gracious to
me, for I am lonely and afflicted. The troubles of my
heart have multiplied; free me from my anguish.
—Psalm 25:15–17

Be merciful to me, O LORD, for I am in distress; my
eyes grow weak with sorrow, my soul and my body
with grief. . . . But I trust in you, O LORD; I say,
"You are my God." My times are in your hands.
—Psalm 31:9, 14–15

The LORD is my strength and my shield; my heart
trusts in him, and I am helped. My heart leaps for joy
and I will give thanks to him in song.—Psalm 28:7

Resurrecting Dreams

The word of God is living and active. Sharper than any double-edged sword, it penetrates even to dividing soul and spirit, joints and marrow; it judges the thoughts and attitudes of the heart. Nothing in all creation is hidden from God's sight. Everything is uncovered and laid bare before the eyes of him to whom we must give account.

—Hebrews 4:12–13

The Lord has a way of looking into the very heart of things—especially the human heart. And there's no use trying to hide what's there.

One day I came to His Word with a nameless ache tucked away inside, troubling me, as it had been for several days. I read Luke's account of Jesus entering the town of Nain, where He came upon a heartbroken widow following the coffin of her only son.

> When the Lord saw her, his heart went out to her, and he said, "Don't cry." Then he went up and touched the coffin, and those carrying it stood still. He said, "Young man, I say to you, get up!" The dead man sat up and began to talk, and Jesus gave him back to his mother (Luke 7:11–15).

As I pondered what this story could possibly have to do with me, the Lord looked into my heart and said, "Something has died in you, Susan. What is this thing you're mourning and carrying in a coffin?"

I was startled, for I hadn't known that a funeral was going on inside me. But He reached out and touched the coffin that I was indeed laboring beneath, and I finally stood still and looked.

An important dream was being taken for burial—a dream the Lord knew I needed to have alive.

Very quietly, from within the depths of me, I heard Jesus whisper, "Do you suppose that if I can resurrect people, I can resurrect dreams too?"

I read the story again and saw the compassion, the power, and the *truth*. When our last hope is being taken for burial, Jesus sees, wipes away the tears of sorrow, and speaks LIFE into our emptiness.

Praise God, He is the Lord of resurrection! The Lord of hope! In choosing Jesus as Savior and Lord, we have chosen abundant, eternal life. And it starts in *this* world.

> *I have set before you life and death, blessings and curses. Now choose life, so that you and your children may live and that you may love the LORD your God, listen to his voice, and hold fast to him. For the LORD is your life.* —Deuteronomy 30:19–20

One Brief Burst
of Glory

Heaven gives its favorites early death.
—George Gordon

Like an annual flower
 she blossomed
in one brief burst of glory,
 dazzling eye and heart.
Designed by her Creator
 for one treasured season of
joy and inspiration—
 then gone—
never needing to know
 sharp pruning shears
nor harsh, barren winters
 and painful, repeated struggles

up through frozen sod to
    gray and weeping skies,
as we perennials must.

Precious in the sight of the LORD *is the death of his saints.*   *—Psalm 116:15*

A Harvest of Thanksgiving

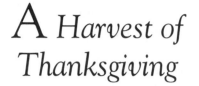

Was anything real ever gained without sacrifice
of some kind?

—Arthur Helps

Our Pilgrim parents came to this continent looking for
a land where they could live and worship in freedom.
They were met with hardship, stark poverty, sickness,
despair, and loss upon loss as they were pitted against
hostile nature.

A combination of exposure, over-exertion, and
inadequate provisions claimed one brave life after
another. Their records show that by March 1621 half
of their remaining hundred had died, "the living
scarcely able to bury the dead."

Yet one by one they carried their precious ones to a field at the summit of a small cliff and buried them there—thirteen of the eighteen wives, more than half of the fathers, four entire families.

Realizing that the Indians must never know the extent of their losses, they did not mark the graves with even a small stone. Instead they planted their grave-field with corn.

We do not suffer as profoundly as our Pilgrim parents, yet we are still afflicted. We too have lost things precious to us—people, health, hopes, abilities, dreams for ourselves and for our children. But instead of planting something of use or beauty over the graves of our losses, some of us have built monuments instead, making it easy for our Enemy to target our areas of vulnerability.

Can we be as brave as our ancestors and baffle the Enemy by refusing to mark the graves of our losses? More than that, dare we convert our cemeteries to cornfields?

Ah, that we may learn to yield a harvest of Thanksgiving from the ground of our losses! It is our rich heritage.

Remember your leaders. . . . Consider the outcome of their way of life and imitate their faith. Jesus Christ is

the same yesterday and today and forever. . . .
Through Jesus, therefore, let us continually offer to
God a sacrifice of praise—the fruit of lips that confess
his name.   *—Hebrews 13:7–8, 15*

"I tell you the truth, unless a kernel of wheat falls to
the ground and dies, it remains only a single seed. But
if it dies, it produces many seeds."   *—John 12:24*

A Tribute to Living

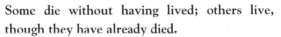

Some die without having lived; others live, though they have already died.
—Unknown

To My Dear Pastor Hart,

I'm forwarding this letter to your heavenly address. Even though you are gone, I need to tell you some things. I want you to know the most important lessons you taught me, both from the pulpit and from your life.

You proved to me that life is best lived in precise, declarative sentences of truth. That such truth delivers best when it is both simple and profound. That truth belabored is truth belittled. I experienced the impact of this truth as you mixed it with humor, enthusiasm, love, commitment, and full knowledge of its authority.

I watched you prove that people, God's Word, and His presence, praise, and love are the only important and lasting things on this earth.

I watched you savor and enjoy all that God brought to you while you were here. I have never known anyone more fully alive while confined to the limitations of humanity and this world.

But God has taken you home now, where you are truly alive. He has left me here. I will carry on.

You left rich resources for the task, for I've not only been taught but also touched and changed by you. I feel the stinging truth that life is short. I feel the prodding truth that my world will not be changed unless I spend myself as you did.

You were a good steward of your *life*—you spent it for the glory of God. I, in turn, will try to be a good steward of your *death*, spending its opportunities for the glory of God.

But I can't help missing you. I'm not ashamed of my tears. I'm so grateful that I told you, just two days before you left us so unexpectedly, that I love you and thank God for bringing you to us. You responded by telling me how much you loved me—loved us all—and how thankful you were that you came here.

You did, indeed, love us. How well named you were. You both lived and died with heart. God gave us His best in you. We'll not waste His generous gift.

Eternal love in Christ,

Susan

Written on the death of my pastor, Hartley Christenson, who suffered a massive heart attack while playing tennis on September 7, 1985, at the age of 49. This book is dedicated in part to his wife and my friend, Marlene.

"He has crossed over from death to life."

—John 5:24

And I heard a loud voice from the throne saying, "Now the dwelling of God is with men, and he will live with them. They will be his people, and God himself will be with them and be their God. He will wipe every tear from their eyes. There will be no more death or mourning or crying or pain, for the old order of things has passed away." *—Revelation 21:3–4*

Creative
Healing

Within every furrow of grief lies a seed of healing.

The holidays just weren't going to be the same without my mother around. She had loved the season so much—the music, the meaning, the decorations, and our family gatherings. I had no idea how I was going to get through them without her.

But then an idea came to me. I don't know exactly when or how it came, but it arrived with an urgency I could not ignore. I had to make a special "Mom Tree."

Never mind that I had a hundred and one things to accomplish before Christmas. Never mind that we already had a fully decorated ten-foot pine in our living room. Never mind that I didn't want even that *one* Christmas tree, let alone *two*.

Yet the thought persisted. Get another tree especially for Mom. Decorate it with her collection of white angels, pink cherubs, and the little white lace fans she had adorned with flowers. Use tiny white lights, a garland of silver ribbon, tuck airy bunches of dried baby's breath into the branches, and make special ornaments.

Make special ornaments? I didn't have time to take a deep breath! How could I take time to shop for materials and design ornaments?

But an out-of-town friend called to ask a favor. They needed trees and decorations for their academy's big holiday outreach program. Would I check out a discount Christmas warehouse near the Mexican border?

The warehouse didn't have what my friend needed, but, as it turned out, they were practically giving away pearl-white balls, silver ribbon, small peach and pink silk roses, and strands of tiny pearls. The ornaments made themselves in my head. They were beautiful. I could see them hanging on the tree that somehow "had to be."

So I let other things go undone and I made orna-ments. I thought about my Mom as I worked—the things she loved, said, and did, ways in which we were alike, ways in which we were different. It seemed we were creating the tree together, for her handiwork and mine hung there side by side. She was, after all, here for Christmas.

Night after night I would stay downstairs after everyone had gone to bed and just sit looking at our beautiful tree—feeling, remembering, letting go, and taking hold. Sometimes I cried, sometimes I smiled. Sometimes I felt Mom was enjoying it too. And then I would laugh at myself, thinking how drab my won-derful tree must look next to heaven's splendor. But it was good. For I was taking time to grieve—cre-atively.

I would never have thought of such an idea myself, but the One who created us in His image knows how to lead us into experiences that will help us work through loss. Perhaps we will find comfort in working on a special garden, scrapbook, video tape, memory quilt, afghan in his or her favorite colors, or a special song, painting, or poem.

But however we work through our sorrow, we can rest in the knowledge that our great Creator offers us the comfort of creative healing, for He is in the center of our sorrow.

As a mother comforts her child, so will I comfort you.
—Isaiah 66:13

I have put my words in your mouth and covered you with the shadow of my hand—I who set the heavens in place, who laid the foundations of the earth . . . Sorrow and sighing will flee away. I, even I, am he who comforts you. *—Isaiah 51:16, 11–12*

He Comes in Winter

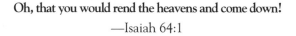

Oh, that you would rend the heavens and come down!
—Isaiah 64:1

> He could have come in
> > springtime
> > > when flowers force their way
> > through sod and
> > > bleating hope is born.
> He could have been spring's Lamb!
>
> He could have come in
> > summer
> > > when sun streams down
> > to warm that hope and
> > > breezes cool the doubts.

Ho, summer's Brightest Son!

He could have come in
   autumn
      when hope flames forth
   with blazing joy and
      crimson paints the earth.
Behold, He's autumn's Glory!

But He comes in
   winter
      when hope lies frozen
   in the night and
      blizzards rake our souls.
He comes, our Living Hope!

You see, at just the right time, when we were still powerless, Christ died for the ungodly. Very rarely will anyone die for a righteous man, though for a good man someone might possibly dare to die. But God demonstrates his own love for us in this: While we were still sinners, Christ died for us. . . . For if, when we were God's enemies, we were reconciled to him through the death of his Son, how much more, having been reconciled, shall we be saved through his life!

—Romans 5:6–8, 10

"I have come that they may have life, and have it to the full."   —John 10:10

Note to the Reader

The publisher invites you to share your response to the message of this book by writing Discovery House Publishers, Box 3566, Grand Rapids, MI 49501, USA. For information about other Discovery House books, music, or videos, contact us at the same address or call 1-800-653-8333. Find us on the Internet at http://www.dhp.org/ or send E-mail to books@dhp.org.